PRAISE FOR *LOVELIKE*

"*LOVELIKE* signals a shining new talent. Sah Pham offers deeply felt poems with a captivating voice that conjures the richness and strength won from bonds between daughters and mothers. These poems are a beautiful exploration of connection and resilience—they operate as a guidebook for how to celebrate our most treasured loves."

—**Rena Priest**, 2021–2023 Washington State poet laureate

"Sah Pham is a poet of strong and haunting presence. A bright voice both vulnerable and courageous in the search for place, acceptance, and love that's real. Her words will move you."

—**Kimberly Hill**, King County Television station manager

"Sah's poetry is an inundation of relentless love, convincing even the most heart-bruised and cynical among us to believe in it again and take a good look at the fissures in our own hearts. She helps us see how if you take away the pain, you're left with an emptier, easier love. But it's the hard love that is the most meaningful and that you can depend on to see you through the most difficult struggles. This is the kind of poetry that makes you ache; the love in *LOVELIKE* is holy."

—**Amy Hirayama**, WITS Writer, Seattle Arts & Lectures

"Sah Pham's *LOVELIKE* is a timely chronology of how love travels through our hearts and souls, capturing all that we share in the world of joy and grief with her poetic voice that speaks for us all."

—**Shawn Wong**, author of *Homebase* and *American Knees*

"*LOVELIKE* is a tender, frayed net for us, the shipwrecks: "Let / this be your raft." As the poems move like tides, Sah Pham carries us through the crevices of a family's migration, languages spoken and unspoken, and heartbreak. These poems will flow and crash through you, a rejection of the finality of drowning. They are a promise we'll find love in our 'shattered parts' and breathe again."

—**Brian Dang**, WITS writer, Seattle Arts & Lectures

"Trying to understand love is like trying to understand the meaning of each breath as we are taking it . . . it's nearly impossible to conceive of the importance each of those movements has on our being. But Sah Pham attempts to follow those subtleties like a dream she is in the midst of both having and interpreting, and she writes each secret, symbolic message as it whispers to her, I believe, to remind her she is loved."

npts at Blooming

LOVELIKE

Sah Pham

Illustrations by Yvonne Tran

♡Sah

CHAMPIONED BY
URBAN
WORD

POETRY
NORTHWEST
EDITIONS

sal seattle
arts &
lectures

The Seattle Youth Poet Laureate is a special program of
Seattle Arts & Lectures in partnership with Urban Word.

ISBN 9781949166071

Published by Poetry NW Editions
2000 Tower Street
Everett, WA 98201

Distributed by Ingram

PRINTED IN THE UNITED STATES OF AMERICA

for my mother
and her oceans & oceans of love

and to all who love

Me at age eight wearing the same handsewn dress that my mother wore when she was at the refugee camp in Malysia at the same age (see page 16)

I PLANTED A SEED

Written in 2011, age eight

I planted a seed at the end of December,
I dug up a hole so small and so tender.
With a kiss and a good luck hug,
I buried it in the ground snug like a bug.

I watered that seed everyday after school,
but all that it made was a small little pool.
I waited and waited day after day,
Soon I got tired and decided to find a new way.

To the seed I sing and dance,
But it still didn't grow not even a branch.

Then one day I read from a book,
It said to take a close second look.
There was nothing growing with frost on the ground,
My poor little seed must have froze there in the ground.

Then I thought to myself and came up with a reason,
Maybe I planted that seed in the wrong season.

CONTENTS

PREFACE
XIII

WHAT $_1$

SHIPMAKERS
3

LOVE AD
7

DEAR DAUGHTER
10

IS $_{13}$

LOVE SURVIVES
15

*LOVE AS
ENTERANCE
WOUNDS*
17

*SWIM LESSONS;
LOVE LESSONS*
18

*MOTHER'S LOVE
MELODY*
19

SYMPHONIES
20

LOVE FIGURINES
21

LOVE ANGELS
23

SUPERLOVE
26

SINCERELY, DAUGHTER
28

LOVE $_{31}$

PANDEMIC LOVE
33

LOVE LIABILITIES
35

*WE COME APART IN
OUR ACTOR BODIES*
36

LOVELANES
38

LOVE LANGUAGES
39

LOVE LATCH
40

LOVE NOTE
41

BIRDS
42

WHAT IS LOVE
43

*WHAT IS LOVE
BUT A SOFT SEA*
48

LIKE ₅₁

? ₆₅

LOVE EXCERCISE
53

*DO YOU LIKE YOURSELF
ENOUGH TO LOVE
YOURSELF*
54

I BELONG DEEPLY
55

MIRAGES
56

SEAGULLS
57

BIRDS &
58

WOLVES
59

EURPHÓRIA IN EXIT
60

SOMEDAY I'LL LOVE SAH
61

BE NOT AFRAID OF WATER
62

LOVE SCRAPS
67

OCEANS BLOOM
68

*SAVE FOR
SUBMERGED LOVE*
70

LOVE DESCENDS
72

*IN DEFERENCE
TO LIGHT*
74

LOVE BLOOMS
75

NOTES
81

ACKNOWLEDGMENTS
83

ADDITIONAL THANKS
85

ABOUT THE AUTHOR
87

PREFACE

I write to you from the center of a paper sea; my poems origamied like bird wings, fluttering all over my walls as I move to arrange them. Since embarking on writing this collection (and drowning myself in its metaphors), my roommates have teasingly, lovingly declared that my side of the dorm must belong to either a mad scientist, detective, or creative genius.

The truth is, this book is about love, but I wrote its contents in the time spans of when I least felt love's presence. This is not to say I am not loved, because I am in an abundance of love— only that I am attempting to understand love in all its complexities.

You may ask, "why love, why *LOVELIKE*?" I was initially drawn to love because I found it to be a linguistically beautiful word—I liked the sound of it. I wondered, for a concept so complex and universal, how we could have no other words in the English language to express it. Even in Vietnamese, I can name only two: *thương* (affectionate love) and *yêu* (deep, passionate love).

I continued to write about love because love isn't easy, and I didn't want to write about something that was easy. I wanted to explore, experience, and express the difficult truths until I could transcend them. I believe love found me when I needed it most, for love begs to be seen, felt, uttered, and understood.

I'll disclaim that I am no love expert. I'm not qualified to speak on love because love is like the ocean, and I haven't sailed the whole ocean. What I can share with you now is how love has uniquely molded me and why I believe love perseveres. In *LOVELIKE*, you may find that my idea of love is not a perfect image; I experience love in seasons: seed, bud, bloom, wilt, soar. When taken together, the chapters pose a single question: what is love like?

1. **WHAT** cradles history, love, and diaspora as one.
2. **IS** explores the love between a mother and a daughter.
3. **LOVE** is . . . love.
4. **LIKE** merges acceptance with condolence to construct a love letter to the self.
5. **?** is what you make it to be.

As you wade through my words, remember: it is not a lack of love that makes us who we are, but it is our efforts to seed stars in the darkest parts of ourselves that make us bloom brighter. Thank you for venturing into the deep with me.

Love,

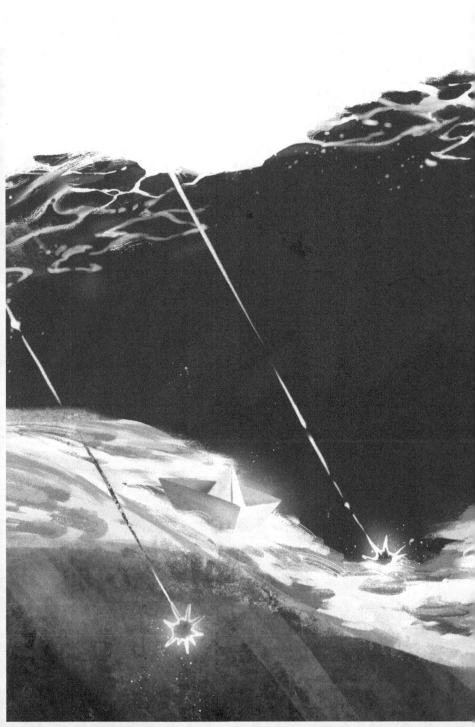

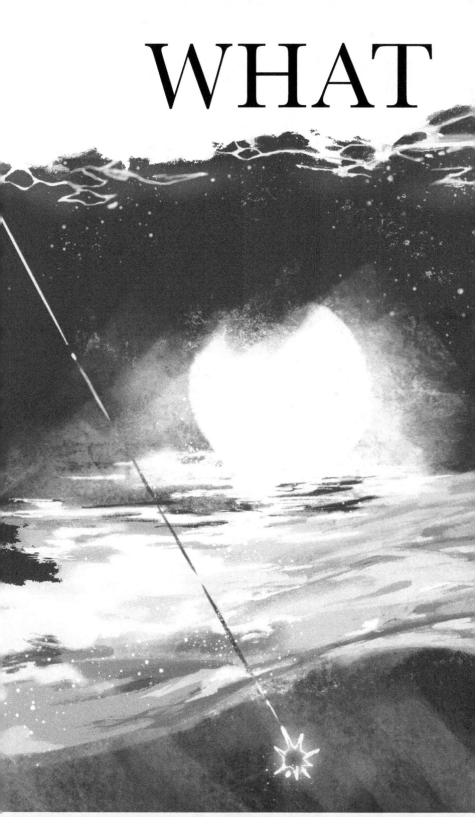

WHAT

SHIPMAKERS

When mother came to land she
in her hands carried

nothing.

The fatherland,
a lustrous wreck of war:
the girl in the picture
running
. . .
burning.

if only my grandmother
understood
the things she photographed
with her eyes

my grandfather,
tinkering with a piece of copper
his callouses,
a topography dated back
—

do we know if he is smithing
a bomb shelter,
or a boatful of stars?

. . .

my mother
takes between stretch of shaky breath her smile
a dream so small you could say
kids are all just dreamers, children of the children of
the landlocked we run to shore
—up all the hurt we fielded
that was not our fault we
paint the sky red
mold a ceramic hand to hold us through

I, daughter of displaced daughter
come to school with
a backpack of water so dense you could have her
paint the sky red / or
learn to swim in cold cathartic ocean / or
return thoughtfully to a verse of history not laced
by sea ghosts or /
maybe teach her
to catch fire
to latch onto this artform
and not this burning body

maybe
sail her back to Saigon before it ends

because

how do you explain heartbreak to a kid
how do you console us who have lost our loveland
looking back over shoulders at a mother that does not properly exist today

I come to school with questions:
how can you still hold me from the other side of this shipwrecked song
how do you mend a beat up sky (paint the sky red)
how can I explain that my Asian-ness is for aesthetic purposes only not to be
tragedied any further

recall that many words are dead in my tongue. I cannot English my way back
into a first language, but
I can at least phoneticise vernacular grief through this verse of art, so

I tell this story
Not because it hurts
Or because I want to illustrate
the art of burning
But because I want to say
thank you.

You taught me
how to catch fire,
How to light a passion project
(and fan the flames)
how to paint the sky red

When the boat catches fire
and it is our turn to kiss the water
breath like a phone on hold

you ask me to write
a part of myself I cannot see
you say, writing is just like boatmaking
And . . . maybe this artmaking could save me

So for the first two decades of my life I
build a boat and sail it to the center of the ocean

sitting silly in a fourth grade classroom
light spills into breath makes voice the same way Mrs. Freeman
guides us into what I now name artful liberation

She says to brainstorm and so I do—
I dance into a tsunami, poeticise hurricane, synthesise the storm
which is to say
in the aftermath of a thousand sunders
we will paint the sky *màu xanh*

Because did you know / the ocean is blue only because the sky is

that when history spilled blood into ocean
We came to America to
paint the sky red
Not because it was abstractly beautiful
But because it was a true reflection

That is why when I come to class
I paint the sky red, and the ocean, too.

I paint for all who swim outside these shores
Who build boats and life jackets and floats
Sowing survival out of reckless imagination
boats big enough to carry our dreams to shore

It is because of this port language,
That I arrive at this pier

Where the same hands before me held nothing
The boatful of stars I hold are burning

So that when I look up
I see that I have everything.

LOVE AD

for the fragmented,
& soon to be whole

I promise
if you are descendants of war

you are chronically
homesick and carrying

millions of dreams
on your back

this poem *can be refuge from the rain*
from the soldiers; from the pain

soldering memories
of an ocean call, of

paris by night re-runs, of Saturday
night lives to celebrate your story

we guarantee, if you buy into this dream,
America may just save you from yourself

and we believe in shipped miracles so
your purchase may help save a sunken

child, cries this war out of being
teaches us how to make home

of someone else's hands
side effects may include but are not limited to

you, humming into the dying receiver:
một ngày sớm—one day soon

you will love, how the sea crashes here
you will watch, as the ocean loves, crash:

they call it a marriage; they call it quits,
they call it what it is / a disaster

poetry will demand, but not guarantee
answers

you will say, "Soldier,"
tell me,
can you colonise

the salt
or does it belong to the sea

for a limited time only
you can buy back shot time

you can witness Saigon
un-wounded, you can watch

how they run, like birds into ghosts
how they swim, eyes open

how they love—through the billows
how they flee—this burning body

refugees, boat people,
my people, can testify

for $1.99, you can buy a figment of heaven
on earth, bodies cradle lungs but,

some part of you will always miss the ocean,
and with it, the crash,

so to love again,
come back to the summer of 1979

where you will see
the sea swallow a paper heart

in the shape of a boat,
chasing shortly after saigon

in pink dusk after,
we all lose the war

after, my mother puts down half her past on a fissured shore
after, she sails a million everythings just to have me, after

the part where we survive and it's all okay
'cause when love sets,

you will feel like missing everywhere all at once so
when the heart breaks for homelands,

let it.

DEAR DAUGHTER

Con gái yêu,
         beloved daughter,

there is a time when you will
forget your mother

the place where you came from
and everyone in between:

"I'm homewrecked, and aching"
you will say, in ALL CAPS, and with vocal fry, you

will make empty promises to your
child-self and lose faith; quickly, or not at all

in the banks of a fire you
don't know the name of

you think it's *lửa* or *love*

and maybe,
         maybe your mother is not / a father but
         a place: a voice inside your heart / the grassy meadow you kneel under / the tulle sky
                  when you're
                                   t-ired,
                                   when you're
                  bored,   when you're
                                                      scared / of the dark,

and so there you will ask me:

what does it mean to be a daughter far from the home our mother's left
who are we to remember where it is we come from

and you will say

I'm flowers / and wilting / on the lawn / I'm / smoking / amnesia
I'm forgetting / where I came from, who I am, what I'm meant to be / where I belong

I'm alone / in my head / again / I'm made from scraps, I ridiculed of myself / a story
In my mind, I am / many universes / made the same / I am parsed to pieces

"Mama! I'm drowning."
(in ALL CAPS): I'M DROWNING IN A LOVE.

"Mama, I'm swimming inside my mind"

"Mama, teach me the tongue I have no name for."

"Mama, its not pretty inside my mind"

because for every aching melody,

there is a past

holding our future: hollow
                                                    & captive

making lakes, weeping mudmounds, where are we running to if not our mother

and her oceans

& oceans

of love.

IS

LOVE SURVIVES

Mama, can you tell me the story of your escape from Vietnam?

It was shortly after the war.

It was 1980.

And my parents, who are your grandparents, decided that they would go ahead and let me go first without them.

You were 8 years old.

And we were in a small dark room.

Ba, your mother, was sewing gold in your shirt seams.

Ong, your father, was in shadows pushing freedom up by its shoulders.

To give me a future is to take that risk and put me on that boat.

So when the Communists started building concentration camps out of sandcastles,

You ran to ship / afloat in Saigon ashes

Sang Vượt Biên sea-songs in tropical storm

Tossed boat and identity into same belly.

Mama, how could you still love water after swallowing an ocean of trauma?

I think when I was first on the boat, and in the storm, the cold water at night flooding through the boat was terrifying. But there was a moment during the boat trip that I was able to come up to the surface, and there I could see dolphins swimming. They say dolphins are lucky.

So when currents pulled you far from home / refugee camp in Malaysia,

You learned to swim between fault lines of seawater and soul;

Became courageous girl gazing at the horizon.

The sea is beautiful in that when I was at camp, I would look out at the sea and I knew that I wouldn't be stuck here forever. And it was hope, because I knew that on the other side of the sea was where my parents were, and that one day I would be able to see them again.

Even when alone,
Sea cradled your hurt.
You—holding onto seaglass,
Your laughter brushed ashore,
Swimming into sunset,
You knew only this: love survives.

Just as the sea has storms and huge waves, but if we're able to harness that energy and ride like the wave riders, the surf riders, we can come safely to shore and enjoy that ride.

So here, floating on salted waters, above shadows
In the places where freedom sails,
I find my mother.

Here, where sea meets shore,
trauma and resilience converge.

My mother at age eight with her
three-year-old cousin at the refugee
camp in Bi Dong, Malaysia

LOVE AS ENTRANCE WOUNDS

I wish I could say it's easy to love mama,

                                    & that loving you[r trauma] comes easily,
the way it's easy to love a gentle sunrise settling over the Malay sea
but your oceans were always tumult-   uous, as was your
                        marriage, as is
                                    me
because
        loving you has made a soft science   of us,
you know a mother's love is the one you keep collecting,

                                        like rain pales, like

fissured sonatas, you will feel

                        loved no matter

the weather   as if pummeling   the red sea with redresses

the same way my   *I love yous*   drop entrance wounds

    in your maiden stitches,   as if   suturing you up, mama,   again

this is how we love: hearts caverning cavities in mouths shouting stanzas.

    I am ashamed to have a father   I   am like you, mama, I love

you   are everything I never was
                            you   are all I will inherit   & become
                    I am my mother's daughter

                        I know Vietnam

        like she does: there, rusted, bulleted, bodied   and gone

        staring at a blank   birth,   the   day
watching our cheekbones sunset into each other the way a prodigy
                    child bends her heart to the bridge   of a song,
see
        how the years cry
            as if, mama,

I cannot wait to grow up and be just like you.

I cannot wait to say:

                                    I love you.

SWIM LESSONS; LOVE LESSONS

the waters callous

> to dynamism

> as you falter

> in its loving crusades

until gingerly,

you will start to ask questions

on how to let breathe

and though you will be

unsatisfied,

your lungs will   flutter

out from under the wings of past lovers

you will be

confused and breathless

di về is to go home. is to run your body

until it   hums,   like a breath held too long

you are catapulted into the sea,

you are not equipped to float

I've survived vượt biển

your mother says, *so I can survive yesterday / and I've survived your father's*

anger, so I can survive   tomorrow /

I was made to survive

I was made

to love, in love nothing but love can permeate my skin

today, I can teach you to swim

so you too can survive   love's riptide.

MOTHER'S LOVE AS MELODY

as a child, you come home every night to an aching violin

your mother plays you odes for bedtime

stories, but sometimes, sometimes they sound more like

elegies, her music always sounds like rain:

Vietnam rain, Vancouver rain, California dreamin', Seattle raining

every night we close the shutters, to *Pachelbel's Canon*

kneeling down inside its blackened crescendos, as you

crawl to rest inside your mother's heart

& in here is where she plays to your afflictions,

she plays the passage of invisible bruises,

she mends them until tender, no longer sore,

you can hear a fire crackling in her hollows,

a soft creak and moan under the fingerboards,

a desire to play sonnets with the orchestra

someday, you say, mama, your strings will

bridge their way home, mama,

one day soon we will sing until we soar

SYMPHONIES

lovebirds in the day
make from the wreckage

                                 pulling heartbeats for

                                        hands,

                                                tied in strings

                        I love what's left of you &
                   I love the mess we made

                              from the thunder,

            friends form constellations, each one a cynthia of stars

        making it rain all over my sheet music

                        and this is my family;

                            & this is my family fissuring apart

we make heart-circles with our wrists

        memories fade and so do fugitives, black holes   pharoahing

us back into   a whittled love,

        a wreckage love,

                        worried love may eat us alive *love*,

                              my family, a soft ceiling

          my mind, a melody   tenoring to our

            hearts, falling as

                  broken wings

                           string the end of a song.

LOVE FIGURINES

this is why I love
over the ocean call

though the years, dressed in tides
may toss and turn in tepid times

letters construe for us folded memories
percolating in the mesh

feeding the void hanging from our heartstrings,
finding passage in our fractured silhouettes

in pining for love, we forget that to be beautiful is to be real
there is hope for your hunger

lost in epenthesis,
searching—for the heart / of a metaphor

and, daughter, when you love you voluntarily pull yourself apart
until you are whittled down to the essence of yourself

do not mistake yourself for kindling
when you are the rain and the weather itself,

when you burn because you / choose love
because you belong to yourself

you are dynamite for the riptides
you are grieving an ocean's rib-cage pulled apart

the shadows are growing wherever you go
stamping out the stars, with their facelessness

and there we were,
cleanly made from fractured poinsettias

we were ruptures fallen from knit holes in the clouds
angels made of snow and sand, pressed to the warmth

even as a child,
you carried us home

as we boat mistletoe in summer
as we carry midnight in a dream

so wear this river like a dress you adore
know there are no prerequisites for love.

(read again, in reverse)

LOVE ANGELS

at dusk, we come out of our bodies   and crawl into someone else's heart
we pray to the gods

as if we are the ones who made them, and in worship run deeper into barren
skies / mama says

praying is never a waste of a girl's lifetime

           she watches us bloom
           frost for fingertips

she says it's cold outside. dress warm

           we put on love as if love's
           the only coat we'll ever need

mama says, it doesn't have to last the season

           we leave bare-shouldered
           and burning

she says *love* is a future tense

           we board a bus and it takes us
           farther from where we came from

in retrospect, roads are dark streams rushing—

loving & unloving & falling out of love & running on gasoline love & making due with love is
a winter season waiting; leaky forms of condensation:

I didn't know the clouds   could be so heavy   with unborn snow

outside, we stare at the faith crumbling under boot and sleeting driveways and melting the
front porch, raining down our cheeks

as we make snowmen of the years, let fall the winter wind as it washes us like a river

I didn't know I could feel like a mistake until I met my absent father, and then one boy slowly after
another, in my dreams, it's always snowing / winter and rivers.

because I'm not easy to love and loving me comes easily, but so does the snow when it's coming apart. because loving me is like loving through an ice bath, is like putting your heart to cold hands and believing they will warm with time

contrary to popular belief,
the shuttle does not give us

bluebirds for guides,
so instead we make   the seasons turn

touch here to open door
inside, I was scared of things, of every- thing,

objects in mirror are closer than they appear

outside the snow was a storm, it made of me torrents so if
you lay down we can make angels of the cold ground,

& daughter, when I look at you, I see halos

swirling in the snow, I feel addlings
as if the warless world is real

love, are you numb again?

inside this world you're slowly fading into the swirl, you're making a mess inside your weather, you're needing to rise out of your body; quickly, get up, you are here for a purpose

you are made to love, so LOVE me,

Love, let rain turn to snow—fall

down as time does, as hail on your lashes and your denim
sky turns to smog, dense enough to desecrate, even the
smallest snowflake
can freeze its way into your heart warm enough
to dissolve all your past participles, and all your persistent
nights

are only fever dreams, melting

Love,

I think angels surround ya

I like the way you melt from clouds and glaze blankets over the earth you've fallen into. how you follow your instincts with each smoky breath. how you're so willing to surrender to the weather

because surviving another winter is another year,

is another year for us to have

we have to learn how people like to love, learn how to love in all conditions, let love persist in the eye of the storm so we wear our heart-shackles as hand warmers, as shuttle-passes, as season's greetings,

we survive the storm inside us because we coax love to life despite everything

we're caught in   a February snow—   *Hallelujah*!

Love is cold,   so cold is   the shadow of   my   storm

Mama & her snow angel says, *It's cold outside. we'll put on some love.*

SUPERLOVE

tomorrow, we will be heroes,
but for today,

we will be philanthropists
carpentrying the night

—& one day,
I'll disciple flowers
and give them to you as we

carve out love in toothless shadows
and make holographs of her hearts
—& one day,
I promise:

I'll move mountains as I
make loving a career as captivating as

counting my reasons for waking
as if glass wounds make paper planes,

make constellations
of future failures
—& one day,
I'm sure

your mornings
will dress themselves   in light years

you'll look back at your life, you'll remain
undisgraced
by the love
staring back at you

love, you have to disciple yourself
as rainbows, as starlight

made victim or villain
given the choice you will
choose

after all,
my eyes swallow stars when it's bright out,
I make it rain with my bird scraps

I disciple the ending you never asked for

I make loving you

a superpower.

SINCERELY, DAUGHTER

dear she who holds me in her womb,
you know all too well all apologies are
sung *thank you*s and *ily*s in disguise so
for every *i'm sorry* I seal with my lips
is 52 cents making its way in the USPS

P.S. it's me, daughter of the unselfish prayer
P.S. i'm writing an antapology in reverse
P.S. it all starts with a confession

confession: this book contains an absence of Love
disclaimer: Love is not anywhere in these poems
warning: I say the word Love many times over

and over, we spend so much time trying to be loved
we do not actually practice the art of Loving

loving, before I was born you were alone
neglected, abused, divorced, pregnant

and, then I fell from the sky and you said:
Love, lovely, let me show you the unsallow sea and everything thereafter

as if you were made for the express purpose of loving me as if
the year of the mare was cause for lining the sheets with fresh bánh xèo is
how we children are waited upon at a hospital restaurant as if

all my mistakes are just second wave miracles
begging for forgiveness

forgive me
for the war inside
it's my fault

imperfect love is salient too
there is always a way

away, you told me,
God gives pieces of his heart away doesn't
entertain the negative side of life
asks us to dance under this
never ending sky of gold
Sah, reach for the stars
we cannot survive on goodwill alone.

alone, I replied. I've only seen Vietnam once.

once, I said,
I'm sorry for all the times we fought
and the lies we wrought

I love you—do you love me, too?

to my mother:
confession: I used to say all the time I did not love
you, as a disclaimer for my messy, faulted stars
warning: my apologies are always shouted

shouted, even when I was in my grave
I prayed that the earth would write us to heaven and

God would have issued our eulogies, and
you'd know that I both Love you and was sorry.

mama, our poetry outlasts grief.
there is a love here that most people can only dream of;

I love you as much as you love me.

LOVE

PANDEMIC LOVE

march

then one day the world sunk shore

april

and we, in bated breath, asked
if there is such a thing as empty, spaceless time

may

falling and waking to an immutable brand of sadness,
we wade through moments we cannot seem to quantify.

june

I'm sorry because

july

when pandemic hit I
tried my sexuality on like a life vest but it did not save me

I spent my summer foolishly,
chasing strangers who did not want me,

august

my first kiss was with a boy who
dotted dark doubts in me; for three months I
became passive in my own story
did you know / words make pockets of shame soft enough to fall into and
stolen touch is dangerous enough to make you feel dirty

september

dear body,
it's not funny when you
shatter
and all you are left with
are your own breathless condolences

october

so when you became sick of love
that never existed in the first place,
you understood that this
is what coming apart in quarantine feels like,
that sometimes,
loving is a form of drowning.
I'm so, so sorry.

And then one day everyone fell sick / but me.
we woke to coronavirus in sleepy grief and I,
I was scared for grandma and grandpa, of
the silence between their coughs,
fits of laughter turned to wind-washed breath
of lungs collapsing under weighted imagination, so for fourteen days
I laid in lukewarm bathwater / counted metaphors in pale dark / siphoned piers of
indecipherable tears and continued on in filtered breath.

I miss the ordinary intimacies,
the syncopated breaths of a thousand strangers,
gentle hugs and inconsolable happinesses.
I remind myself that, like pain,
this too will subside in deep water,
receding as ocean furls fingers into fists / crashing waves
Let it wash away any semblance of shame, for
I am still learning to pick up my own shattered parts,
to surrender them to weathered sunrises and
distant dreams because

there is a light, I can see it
peeking over our horizons and
shuttered glass panes.

LOVE LIABILITIES

Merge south under the orange-skin sky, take the fast lane
In the absence of material bodies, yours is the first exit

slight right, cruise by / a / feminine Mercedes / a / bisexual Toyota / a / slut-Bug
the horizon coppers itself chrome

In my periphery your life slams into mine
Hit the brakes—a pickup cuts me off

slowly, we do not love each other
I have always had leather skin for seat covers

four way stop: you have the right-of-way
we yield chafed breath gone tire flat, nothing to

say, I shut off the stereo, and with it, our song hey
"Spotify, can you please play me a song away from here"

TAKE fast lane, first EXIT, slight right, hit brakes, SLOWLY,
crash into your lover's ghost then

when collision cleanup comes I
gather all the airbags in my body scream

obscenities because you handed me your ghost in the backseat of our last collision stash my
sickness in the cup holders and demand pieces of you at the drive-in

laugh at the pedestrians because you are perhaps the purest part I have ever crossed out inside
myself let the world blank into contraflow and high-lanes, citrus melon and flimsy directions

drop my smile on the gas and lift my third finger out the sunroof
switch the floodlights on and kiss the speed limit

run myself through a car wash, seatbelts sweaty

I forgive the broken road.

WE COME APART IN OUR ACTOR BODIES

I feel lilies in my stomach, curling in on the stars.

The stage is alight with emotion. I could fall asleep in these opera chairs.

And not that it matters but I feel wrecked from the inside out.

"Why are you re-wounding yourself?"

Because the music takes me back to the forest we parted in. I could make our friendship alive again with my voice. But the way things ended was never enough. Because when the fire remakes itself, it burns out, if only for a moment. Your laugh ashes all the joy in my bones. When you say my name I no longer recognise myself. The girl you're looking for is gone,

and so I hang up the phone and put down my heart.

Years later, you will see that the story you tell yourself is not always the truth. Believe me. This play is a paper set, with paper lights, and paper walls, and paper feelings, ready to blow over at any moment. Because all you feel when you awaken a death is nothing, because nothing is the same. People move on when you want them to. Stars are only wounds for so long until they ascend—black holes tendering in on themselves. All matter is gravity pulling so much weight, even light cannot escape your grasp.

I am trying to method act. I am attempting to bloom a masterpiece from emotional ashes.

So you take everything in. You believe everything is your fault. You think deeply about every masterpiece you create and conclude that things could have ended differently. You feel the same hurt as the people whom you hurt. You hand the world what it wants. You feel dressed in dirt and soil and need more watering. You lack the light and beg some lamp to shower you in goodwill. The heart begs to be broken again. In the backdrop, the stars fall limp and make little splashes denting dimples in the ocean, splitting us in two. And this is the part where the main character hurls herself into a patch of feeling, because feelings are all she knows.

The director says: never apologise for loving somebody. And so this is the moment where the whole world falls in love with a broken bird, as it begs for understanding. You forgive the earth and thank it for holding you, watch the dawn as it unfolds and know how the dusk hurts. But these will all be blips in my memory. They will only be puddles to cry out the storm. I give you permission to close the mouth of this burning bridge. But so you should know, I'm in a better place now, I'm counting down the stars. In my bombshell state, I want to know if these feelings are real, or if I'm just acting.

LOVELANES

I'm told I ~~love~~ swim too delicately;
coach says my strokes are

    beautiful, but

swim harder, like you're not afraid
of water

    so you'll see that

when swimming quickly
you're not submerged

you're skimming—
body barely under wave,

beyond breath

so that this is my body pushing against itself;
is letting love abandon it slowly, relinquish
racing to obscure the dimming, the dauntless

as if water and breath belong in the same poem
deserve to be on the same page

but so you should know,
like love,

swimming is a survival sport

we race lane
              -lines and love
                       -lanes
not for strength or speed,

but endurance.

LOVE LANGUAGES

because loving is all / my body / was born laughing

I think it must have learned to love
in another lifetime, until it became muscle memory

like language, love remains potent in the arsenal of human imagination
and like love, our language knows not how to articulate itself

so we try not to start sentences with *love* or *lovable*
we try not to verb-alise *love* because admitting to love is scary

and so instead we come away with twisted tongues or shut mouths
but still we run to love even as we cannot fathom the words

love speaks its language for us, through us, by us
so with the time we had, as the people we were

with our hopes and our dreams and everything
we were, wanted, could never be, already are

love conspired till it had us by lip-lock and hand-hold,
had us by starry eyes and bent good-byes

so much so that with you, everything has languisized, into a particular loving, where loving
has become a language, and it remains a language long after we have stopped speaking it

even though words have ceased to be spoken between us
and love is not something to be articulated between us,

even after we have neglected this language,
even as it is an extinct language,

it is one we remember to carry with us

LOVE LATCH

when we are lonely,
                when we are sad
when we are bored
                of the things we cannot remember
when we want someone
                to confide in
when we have no one
                to lean on
when we are mad at
                each other
when we are sorry
                for how things ended
when we are sick
                with dreaming
when we are tired
                of ourselves
when we lie awake
                at night
when we search
                for stories
when we look
                for ghosts
when we have cried
                in waking
when we ask
                questions
when we start
                to misbehave
when we have
                given up
when we interlace
                our fingers
when we come
                together
like the hands
                of this poem.

LOVE NOTE

I hope you'll one day forgive me for breaking your heart; and yourself, for being heartbroken. That you'll relinquish yourself of the burdens you carry. Hurt lasts a lifetime but so does the opportunity to fall in love again. What you had with me you will have the gift of experiencing over and over again. You will break hearts. They may break yours. This will all happen consensually, because love is and love does and love gives and love takes and love hurts and love bends and love breaks. I know you understand this, and intimately. I know this because I love how you love, how you embody love; that if you continue to love, the world will reflect your love.

I know the ocean never stops swallowing the hearts of the hurting, but it continues to love all who swim its waters, anyways. In the weeks after I returned your heart, I felt debilitated. I experienced a feeling of weakness like I'd never felt before. Even though I knew it was you who should be hurting more, I blamed myself for all the improbabilities. And in the absence of your love, I forgot how to love myself. Because no one feels strong after they break up.

So let love love, and let love hurt. You can grieve, but try not to grieve grieving. Don't beat yourself up for being human. Go gentle. Don't stop loving the concept of love just because someone declares love's over between you. You will always have a place in my memory, and a couch to crash on in my heart. Just because the game ends, doesn't mean the players stop loving. What we had isn't gone—it loops, infinitely, in the past, making memories of love limitless. And love that's settled between us? That was only a moment of love expressed in a single relationship. There are so many more instances of love, god-given, that we can hold in our breaths, over friends and over lifetimes.

I look back on our time together and feel oceans of gratitude. I know you feel the same. I just hope one day soon, you'll reclaim yourself, as I'm attempting to do with the missing parts of me still lost in love's tides. So I'm letting you go. It's okay to let me go, too. Put down the phone, this letter, your hurting, and come back out into the world. You're going to be okay. If you love Love, it will love you right back. I promise.

BIRDS

I think I finally understand
why birds, set free, soar.

over the snowcaps
they carry my

dead parts

bruises, let down, gracefully.

when you love someone,
you set them free.

WHAT IS LOVE?

Love is
an anomaly.

is / the part where
you watch

as the ocean glows,

swallows your mother

as it

to the soundtrack of   America

home.

is / the part where   you watch

laughing

at the war / and calling

politely ask you

as the friends you considered friends

abandon ship   and

to drown

is / the part where   phantoms

follow you home and

with them.

make fun of your name, your

all you can do is   clothes,

the place where you came from   and

save what's left

is / the part where

you watch a man

on the television   shoot

of yourself.

is / the part where
you look at   in the heart.

old   photographs and realise   is displaced
                                         your family   your future child

lost at sea, and some have   living forever rent free

is / the part where
                    PTSD   in the form of some elephant
            you watch   as your middle school principal
grows a garden out of a school and /   a decade later, leaves   because
                                she's an Asian woman
                                         with a brillance
                                racism has no tolerance for

                    in high school
is / the part where
the white girls would   whisper   in the halls and   talk over you,
            when
no one paid attention   because you   couldn't be extorted or   leveraged so
            you were worth   abandoning   is / the part where
a year later,
            you finally have the courage to   call   an old   friend   and
                    nothing,   and then:
all she has to say is:
"goodbye" and "you'll find your people" and also "it's so weird you're still thinking about me because I forgot all about you" and so
after that,   you   hang up the phone   and you   realise   it's not because
you tried but   because she never cared   in the first place   so you finally see that

this is not love,
an amalgamation of your vulnerability, it never was
love, it was just pretending, it was just
there exists certain people in this world and
sometimes it's nice to know that
you have that and you get the choice not to be one of them,
they refuse to act in love / you are strong choice, to be better / to love when
for people who because you choose
who exemplify love because to be love,
you are Love, you become Love, you choose to love Love,
are Love,
even when love fails you
sometimes,
I think you
have so much love to give and
no one to receive it well, because some people
don't know how to handle
Love, they learn they'll how it's fragile
and still it's
inside you and twist it till it crush hurts what's left of it
when you when you can't sleep
think it's your fault you weren't good
enough not loving enough, your love not your lovely enough so
to Love is to love even as you watch

the absence of love
wither by the seaside,

as you watch

your

dreams

fall asleep in someone else's flames and

call it

"love," and you

still you

run to it

no matter

how many times it

burns you

because

LOVE

Love,

true love,

is anchored in you when

you feel unlovable, so

when you feel unlovable

let

this be your raft.

Let your love for Love

be your mother,

and know,

hurt

that no matter by how many measures love burns you,

it can't

know you

like

you

Love does,

I promise

because you don't

and after all this, you will still ask:

                                                        / like God does

"WHAT IS LOVE?"

                                        and well, love is an anomaly
                                        what you make of it.

So no matter what,   promise me this:

you have to love people   even when
        they're hard to love /
        you have to try

                        to love love again /
                                to not give up on loving love /

to love even when people   don't deserve loving   even when

love breaks you

even when they are selfish / and cruel / and they'll leave you /

l o v e l e s s,

you must love like you've never known love's absence   before.

WHAT IS LOVE BUT A SOFT SEA

where bodies of water sanctify

love languages:

the dive-block, a love ledge
                                        -ible to find footing in

my sorrows, the currents
                            continuing to hold me as

bodies, bombing the water, shelled softly,

                            we are head-first diving
into a dream

enter: the water, fiercely & cleanly

        like a bird,   sub-marined

I can trace my finger 'long love's currents; I find no edges

to scar me

& this is how I swam out
from under my fingertips

the world washed in, I
fell from wings I forgot

how to fly,

slamming hearts & slamming doors,

people watching,
        through leaking panes

as if phantom to my voice
        in a dress—wearing lungs

shaping breaths   I waded through ache

& anchored lullaby,   I splashed as I mourned

swimming until   swollen

though heavens fall into

                         lane lines

              and love lines

                         us up at the shore

be assured:
you are not alone

              —only lonely, sometimes,
              but loneliness

can be gutted

              there is always some

                              -body calling your name,

some ghost to settle for
              the night will not be empty:

it will be a hatchery of all things *dream*

it will be mercy and minnow and miracle

cause skinny love [in brackets] and
              [in lane-lines] makes us thin enough to starve,

paperless enough to be surrendered, fragile

and buoyant—   enough ripple to fade

as the salt makes the burn grow brighter

with every uncharted breath

you take

LOVE EXERCISE

Close your eyes.
Press   your palms   to the sky and reach into the dark
on the other side, there is this feeling of nothing / you may like
yourself better this way. Take your anger, smoking the skies

                                      dull, your
doubts, montaging masterpieces of self-

                         affliction, made merciful your
insecurities, redressing themselves in your

                         clothes.
Take the days you felt

                         empty

as the room inhaled & exhaled with rattled

                         wind. Don't forget the rain tinting your car

windows. The melody of others making you feel less

                         than you are. Lodged at the base of your throat is

a cough drop. Take your exhaustion, your sad, your quiet, your heaviness, your not-enoughs,
your frustrations, your burnt-out

                         scars,
                         Here.
open your palms.

Toss it in the ocean. Aim for the mouth. Waters will swallow whatever you feed it / call it

                         catharsis.
now, run back to find your child self:

The first-grader sitting alone in a classroom. The nine-year-old crying in your bedroom. The
twelve-year-old—fists closed, and heart, too.

Witness yourself with open palms.

Hug little you.

DO YOU LIKE YOURSELF ENOUGH TO LOVE YOURSELF?

& trust me, I've tried

everything.

all the panaceas of the world, I've sutured & sculpted

"self-love" only to

lose myself constantly

'cause the world will do everything it can to sell you

everything

that is not love

& love that is bought, love that comes at a price

buys nothing

so understand this is the life I give you. do everything you can. stray every chance you get.
being unsure and uncomfortable and unknowing is what will eventually make you gorgeous

-ly dangerous.

but know that growing pains make no promises:
you'll compare yourself with who you could be.
you'll waste countless hours trying to be enough and it will not be a waste / but a lesson

a call to see that everything was perfect all along.
that we all come into this world upside down.
that we have it backwards all the time and refuse to see it.

So here is what will happen:

There's a little life I want you to live: no promises, no rules, no
obligations, only love.

If you're confused, remember who you are. Hold onto your name. Don't worry too much
about how things ended and focus on beautiful beginnings. Make your life useful, your hands,
too, and your voice: everything in you is bound to be saved, if you would just let love save you
from yourself. Be love, & love will guide every action you take.

I BELONG DEEPLY

excruciatingly
lovingly   impossibly
         burningly
        beautifully
          unabashedly
            uncontainably
              unmistakably
         completely
                effervescently
          effortlessly
              miraculously
                hopelessly
                truthfully

                      unabridgedly

to myself.

MIRAGES

if it's not love, don't water it

it doesn't matter if you have acne, or bruises, or scars

read this when you feel ugly.

as if being pretty is a prerequisite for being seen;

a call out to make the gods feel unsure
                                        of their creation

of your existence,
            just enough to be famous:

we are apostrophied in our (lack of) breath,

cacophonied by

            intuitions.

trust makes you who you are so

come back to yourself in the same way you return to slumber

please don't let the absence of a good thing ruin anything else.

you are lost. you are searching. for answers you may never find.

                    feel the wind
                            through your shields
            close your eyes

I know how it feels to be alone in yourself

for after all this, your moments will be whittled down

to mirages / damned to disciples of the dark.

SEAGULLS

are white skinny chickens that can fly

& sometimes, sometimes you think you can, too, so wake up, your stomach flat / torso toned as a river / you think / you should be content by now but / you're late for class and everything else

yesterday, when impulses didn't rescue you burned hours and slept when the world woke / sleepy you sat on the couch and listened because you couldn't get up, you didn't want to

meanwhile, you continue to run back to the idea of men; you are torn between loving and giving up on them as you origami your hands into new folds you contemplate the juxtaposition of life

asking for recompense, like a daughter smoothing out failures you think all this time you're burning is wasted / but nothing is wasted drifting between alive and

tired; internalising falsehoods cemented under burberry sky what will my body be if not / a constellation of birds / begging to break free, / forgiving us of place and time

for my body cannot process what it does not know, it can only escape temptation, because only my body knows who it is / and so it is only when we exit ourselves, that we become chickens

that can fly.

BIRDS &

human limbs are intricately composed

of a mesh of densities

confused as fragile or unbreakable,

someday the scientists and poets will

abridge each other, they will say to

let every bird break you so

that bird by bird, wingbeats turn to

phantom limbs, you will live to free love

from its solitudes, mask the stars'

messy existence, we are falling

into holes we dug with our foot-soles

in the sky, black stars collapsing inwards

for this is how the body learns to love itself

as it takes the wingspan of a song

WOLVES

you are a room of ruminations / you're staring into / dark corners again / begging love to land back / on the porch. listening to the cicadas church out a summer, staring / at the constellations / making / empty promises: hearts / breathing, the ground / beating / as we chase a burning sparrow / to be fatherless / is to be a wolf / awake in the night, guarding your mother / from the hunger / of wolves / hunting / what we started / we mend the wreckage and / satiate the hungry / void / in the centerfolds / of the heart, / we make the quiet life / worth living / we make storms / raised by hungers / in the depths of nights / what happens when you pray is / birds / bombing heart / beats into / heaven / into the mouths of sharks / that look like dogs.

EUPHORIA IN EXIT

you exit the pool and into the night &
when you think of yourself   you think: *she could never be as beautiful as*
she is   *when*   *she is in her era.*   when the
night engulfs her in   euphoria.   when   her friends corral her back   to
earth and   remind her   she is worth   eulogising over.   that her   joy
is   *so pretty.*   that her love   for everyone   and everything
is so tantili-   zing.   that she is   worth something   in her
skin.   that she is   flame   for the   moths.   that
everyone sees it   but her, / so   eyes are   not really the problem
here is my night.   here is my   water-   fall.   here is the laughter
drifting out of   the gallery bar and   into the elevators,   into my
front door   ,   into my room-   mates   making me   less alone   again
in   my thoughts   is a quiet place. is a soft sanctuary to watch for.   are all these
strangers   hungry   for a story.   hungry to be heard   in the name of
acquaintanceship, in the name of love, in the name of: "today, I will finally belong to
someone who   reciprocates   my sight."   today, I can   forget
my thoughts and   be in the light.   today I can be tired
and sleepy and   it's all   okay. its all   meant to be   okay.
because   we will be okay tonight.

-rah, *xít vô, xít ra*
scoot in, scoot out

giống như sóng biển
like how the waves *ra vô*
roll in and out
hình ảnh ngươi me
a mother image
niềm vui và nỗi buồn
happiness and sorrow
của
belonging to
người con
bé
your body
is
little
tears are
only the beginning
of your story
Sah ơi,
không cần phải xinh đẹp
you don't need to be beautiful
để có tình yêu
to have love

Sah-uh,
I see your future
descending into
your hands.
Take it.

SOMEDAY I'LL
LOVE SAH

Sah ơi, Sah-uh
là trên trời rơi xuống
you are from sky fallen

Sah, I know you said you
feel alone, but
know there will always be
angels around you
Sah ơi, I will always love you
Sah ơi, I will not let you collapse
Sah, remember you are dust,
and to dust
you will return
Sah, remember
what you were inscribed
on this earth to do

Sah, hold onto your name.
for if you let go, you will
lose the sounds of yourself,

and remember, even if
your melody is marred

I promise your name is a lyric
it will boat you home
safely and to shore.

BE NOT AFRAID OF WATER

and this is how I love: breath for breath
like waves—*crashing* / & waves rising

tides, be not afraid of loving, of people
watching, because how I love is:

laughing, sitting side by side / & saying
nothing, but still feeling, even if love's

raining, if love's pouring / if love's
looking for love & love's flowing

out / from under us, if love's acquitted
& alone by the pool -side, fingertips

gracing the surface like a bent dive
you will swim side by side

you will survive; sinking & swimmers
pools of light & shadow, sodden

you will give breath and you will
take breath and you will leave breath

behind, & again you
will become breath   -less,

besides,

a body of water is only a body
until it livens to become *lover*

when you learn to be un-afraid of water
you will become bolder

you will not sink beneath the

riptide, you will learn to love falling

in love is like synchronised
swimming, is like staring into empty

abyss is like *diving* in
the deep end is love
                          -ing until your

breath begins pouring,
you will keep swimming,

life is the space suspended between
the ledge and the ocean-bed

breath for breath / love
is like lungs surfacing, is laughter

lifting, puddles shallow enough

be not afraid of breaking

love's surface / is the only way to
remind your breath to breathe again.

LOVE SCRAPS

1. You spend your whole life swimming only to never reach the shore.

2. We are in quiet company. We startle the stars.

3. You ask for contemplation, coming from the mouth of the torn.

4. The tides turn with each breath, each stroke a new wave.

5. Don't feel like you have to suffer so much just to arrive as you are.

6. All that passes through you is like water hitting a ghost on an immovable shore.

7. A pool of regret can only be filled for so long before it drains you.

8. Someday all your mistakes will be micro-miracles melting in someone else's heart.

9. It's almost miraculous how we can create inner worlds out of nothing in particular.

10. How all this raw material is wasted. How after cashing in on your education all that is left is the bone marrow you started with. How when you plan your funeral the outcome is songbirds in the night and you will never know.

11. You will never know how rainbows rain after the starlight. How I miss you dearly.

12. I'm sightseeing again because I like to believe that good things require personal development. Has anyone ever told you that you're incredibly beautiful?

13. That when dreams fade our friendship will sustain the dark. How after everything that has happened and everything that never will, something lasts. A little longer than we intended it to.

14. It survives the reptile inside us. The monster under the bed remains asleep because we treat it well. Our feelings stay dormant in a chorus of vocal fogs. The fray is not too far away.

15. 'Cause the person you are is not who you know yourself to be.

16. When it's dark. When I have no one left to lean on. Because the thunder calls me by name and the undercurrents roar ransoms.

17. Do you ever wonder how memories remake themselves? How friends are amalgamations of your past catching up to you?

18. The way everything changes before anything is set in motion.

19. You fall, sideways, into the lesson you needed to witness.

20. You laugh in bucketfuls, love till you forget your footing, make drumbeats of miracles, lay your tears out to dry.

OCEANS BLOOM

I want to believe in the good of people, but all I see is
rain, falling as birds—

everywhere, I make choices

of who I want to be
        because who am I
        but a relentless process of *becoming*

unburdened, bountiful
        are the birds, fluttering
        my breath away,
                making winds of goodwill

because here are my pocket birds, lining my life
across the water, dimplish wounds gushed open under the sea

like how salt wounds collided / in summer /and I was born / from the bay where the war is
won we / pray, counting down the days, making tugboats of love and loving

you, a torrent of winds

birthed and blushed open

So what we do is we burn all the wildflowers
we get suckerpunched in the gut
we climb into the mouth of a monster and
chrysanthemum of ourselves
a fresh day, frayed & fragmented, piece

together a tender, salvaged love

'cause you can leave a place, and
you can leave a person,
you can even leave this world but
you can never leave behind yourself,

—don't give it all away

'cause the truth is, there is no truth

but your own
the same way oceans bloom
turntables

'cause what am I if not nothing? if not the sky opening up to swallow me whole. if not the
failure of a daughter parsing herself to pieces. if not the girl everyone betrays.

because oceans well
and love leaks
foams mouth
stars sink scars bruise billiards, & buoys me home

'cause you arrived when I was most in love with my life
& you loved me so fervently I forgot how to love myself

so we dance to the sounds of ourselves until we forget the music
we pray with our bodies / until the music sings us alive
we move with our mouths on melody, in myriad tragedies,

sing your song until you forget the sounds of yourselves
as you lyric voice into verselessness

You are worthy of experiencing all that is you

so put down the phone.
you know, girlhood is only a setting sun / sinking
beyond the void until one of you gets it right,

until you figure out where you stand in the world
is not the same place where you weep by the wayside

'cause it's gorgeous and tragic inside
but only because no poem can be the beginning or end for us
clutched to gratitudes graces

we will have loved each other in infinite lives—in the past, memories stay whole
& memories continue to live as the past lives on without us, therefore, we are infinite and we
are temporality at its frailest
which makes us wonder
if we are entering daylight or coming out of it
makes us ask from whom before us have we learned this love from

SAVE FOR SUBMERGED LOVE

making mouth meshes of a cylinder sky

you can think of love as everywhere or nowhere, either way, love is

like a fever dream
                you can't wake up from

and this is the story of our *sung xương* (bone marrow)

ocean is love at its most articulate, this is love after all

though we have to ask, is this love at all

because what will I have made with my life, but two empty hands

who am I but a paper daughter, floating in paper-ships we

charter breath-boats and swim ashore

make of love fresh bird scraps;

love scraps   parsed
                            to
                        pieces
                                                        of

                                                            pain

Listen not to what I say, but to everything I do not say

make waves with retribution,
            sow solace from tender times

because one day, I believe we will belong somewhere

and sometimes, I don't know what i'm writing, but it's okay because you understand me.

So here is life. and here is what life could be.

throw everything you have been, will be, and never were.

don't worry about your skin, for skin will fade

and your starlit scars, too

your worth needs no predicating

so you'll find me swimming, delicately, but alive

'cause these poems will make of us angels

holding us by the wings

and submerging the corridors

with a love so buoyant

it may just save us

from dreaming of the dark

LOVE DESCENDS

like a promise

composed over generations

sung over sanctuaries

of our cries

a cacophony of cradled breaths

bloomed by the oceanside

for all you must do

for love to descend

is hold onto your history

—because you should know:

this is how we moved

through the years

our hearts, merged to minutes

as love's descendants

we chartered sailed-breath & tug-ged

blessings, loitered lullabies, as artifice   of anchors

to ground us to ourselves, made brief a   life-line, drifting free of faults

—and you should know,

nothing (save for everything)

can hurt me

'cause I'm descended from

my mother

and my mother's mother

women who have endured   &

waded worse,

    —and here's the harbor:

      a knife balanced precariously over the kitchen sink

like a metaphor, waiting

to skin open the surface of our stories

like fruit

slicing forgiveness for freedom

until you see that I am

my mother's daughter,

we are a lineage of daughters surviving

someone who loves us

belong to a legacy of love

forged through centuries' tides

wound up by ocean's graces

'cause we're scrapped daughters

we're made of fissured love

we're made whole.

IN DEFERENCE TO LIGHT

all my love life is blanks and rivulets
sentences born from swallowed birds
dancing 'long freedom's folds and faultlines

as poetry percussions my exhaustion
holds me 'til all the hearts clink and break

makes me less alone in myself
folding my shadow in tides until
I'm no longer a falling disappointment

because I want this poetry to feel like dancing
I want these bird beats to become winged melodies

and so what is love if not repentance

because loving is like losing
your whole breath
to a song
you didn't write
but you know by heart

& you're not sorry
to have lost yourself
for once in your life
to a spoken song
to a bird's light

for what is the work of love if not
montaging
memories
and making
miracles
of our lives

so in deference to light,
I love you because
love is light

and light will wash away all our loveless parts.

LOVE BLOOMS

In response to "I Planted A Seed"

You can plant a seed in December
and it may not grow but

the seeds you carry today
will be the stars that bloom

tomorrow, and when the
snowcaps melt, you can watch as

bird by bird, seeds fall like rain
making it pour with our love languages—

water-washed, breath-washed, love-washed
away, 'cause *Love*, if love

doesn't grow in this season,
love will bloom in the next

and if seeds of love fail to find you,
remember: only love can hurt like this

'cause only love can grieve like this
and only love can bloom like this

carried over generations
and merged to bird baths

love at its breaking is seed at
its splitting, shedding like onion skins

burrowing roots in the earth
to spring up love's legacies

so you can plant seeds of love
or you can plant seeds of pain

seasons of love make every ending
the birth of a new beginning

know that if you plant love in the wrong season
be assured that love grows wherever you go

that the seeds you plant today
will be the seeds that bloom tomorrow

love's been buried in you all along

because what are we if not bottomless
is love's roots not infinities deep

and so then,
maybe something grows
where our seeds are buried,

that prettier things are made
from the recycled memories

of the ashes rained down,
slated into a turning tide

after all, did you know that
the meaning of love is

contained inside you

so that when you plant words of love
love will bloom all around you.

NOTES

"I PLANTED A SEED" was my first published poem. It won a National Poetry Month award in 2011, when I was eight years old, and was featured in *Seattle's Child*. It is included here: https://www.seattleschild.com/six-winning-young-poets-give-meaning-to-national-poetry-month/.

"SHIPMAKERS" contains a line about "the girl in the picture," which refers to the photograph taken by Nick Ut of Kim Phúc running naked through the war-lined streets of Vietnam. It is also after the title of the book *The Girl In the Picture: The Story of Kim Phúc, the Photograph, and the Vietnam War* by Denise Chong.

"LOVE SURVIVES" was written in KUOW's *RadioActive* Youth Media online radio journalism workshop, with production support from Lila Shroff. It was edited by Kelsey Kupferer and aired as "A poem for my mother, a Vietnam Boat Refugee" in the summer of 2020. Read and listen here: https://www.kuow.org/stories/a-poem-for-my-mother-a-vietnam-boat-refugee.

    Vượt Biên translates to the ocean passage endured by hundreds of thousands of Vietnam boat refugees between 1975 and 1995. Not all who sailed made it to shore.

"LOVE ANGELS" borrows the lyric and melody: "I think angels surround ya" from the song "Wish on an Eyelash" by Mallrat & The Chainsmokers.

"LOVE NOTE" is the letter I never sent. The line "no one feels strong after they break up" is from my roommate Jessica.

"I BELONG DEEPLY" is inspired by the line "I belong deeply to myself," which came from my roommate Myra. It is also found in Warsan Shire's poem, "Excuses For Why We Failed At Love."

"SOME DAY I'LL LOVE SAH" is after Ocean Vuong, Frank O'Hara, and Roger Reeves.

"LOVE SCRAPS" and *"OCEANS BLOOM"* take inspiration from Ocean Vuong's "Notebook Fragments" and Warsan Shire's "Bless this House." They are made of scraps of unfinished poems/fragments of love—short moments/glimpses of love, or lack thereof—not written perfectly or as beautifully as I'd like them to be, or formatted exactly as I wanted them, but nonetheless they felt important to my love story, so that perhaps one day I can come back and try to decipher them.

"LOVE BLOOMS" is a response to *"I PLANTED A SEED"* and was written and performed at the 2023 Seattle Arts & Lectures Gala, "Words Bloom."

ACKNOWLEDGMENTS

A shipful of stars to all who sailed with me in the making of this book:

Seattle Arts & Lectures
thank you for giving my poetry a pier

Vicky Edmonds
for conjuring in my poems briefs of beauty
I am so grateful for how our words bloom

Arianne True
for your breathless brilliance, candor, and genius
your guidance has given me the grace to trust, fly, and fall

Sasha taqʷšəblu LaPointe
for guiding me into trust-fall with my words

Indira Dahlstrom & Jennifer Lobsenz
your bright, enduring presence is a gift

Yvonne Tran
thank you for answering my call and voyaging alongside me
in your art I see dreamscapes; you are talented beyond seas

Cara Sutherland
for laying out my words, like stars, on the page

Wei-Wei Lee, Kendall Kieras, Bitaniya Giday, & Neko Smart
for being poetry, for being friendship, and
for writing, ranting, and laughing with me

Aamina, Abby, Adhya, Bayla, Caden, Diane, Keegan, Kenyon, Kiana, Kyle, Natasha, & Rowan
for being the liveliest, funniest, and of course, most poetic cohort
thank you for inspiring me monthly

Myra, Irene, Jessica, Tracy, Riti, & Arjun
you are a love I imagine siblings sustain
I miss you like crazy

Kathryn
for over fifteen years of friendship
your laughter is childhood at its most loving

my friends, past and present
you know who you are
thank you for your love

Ông Bà & Family
vì thương yêu con, chăm sóc con, vì thương yêu con va chăm sóc con

Dì Trinh   Mama & Lee
you started it all, thank you for   always being there for me
raising me up always   on my darkest days
and for refusing to give up   on us no matter the patches
                this book aspires to your love

& to the countless others who have graced me with your light.
Thank you for believing in me, for seeding stars in my dreams and lifting me up to your love.

ADDITIONAL THANKS

to Ocean Vuong
for making the poetry of our mothers eternally gorgeous—you make me feel seen; your words
continually write me back into existence.

as well as Warsan Shire, Natalie Wee, Tyehimba Jess, Franny Choi, Thi Bui, and many more of
the poets and authors I have had the pleasure of reading over the last three years—thank you
for leading the way and making literature the loveliest it can be.

to the Spotify algorithm, for accurately curating the playlists that kept me company on far too
many late nights and early mornings. More, ahem, people, could learn a thing or two about
emotional intelligence from you.

and with most gratitude,
to the authors, writers, and teachers who have witnessed my work in advance of publication:
Kim Hill, Kelsey Kupferer, Brian Dang, Anastacia-Reneé, Clara Olivo, Amy Hirayama,
Shawn Wong, Rena Priest, and Vicky Edmonds
—your support wells oceans of gratitude in me.

ABOUT THE AUTHOR

Sah (also known as Sarah) Pham is the first Vietnamese American Youth Poet Laureate of Seattle. Her poetry has been featured in *Seattle's Child*, KUOW 1340 AM radio, and the University of Washington's *The Monologues*. She is the founder and former host of *Poemcast*, a poetry podcast at *The Daily*. She has served as a Youth Ambassador for the Bill & Melinda Gates Foundation, youth producer with *RadioActive* Youth Media, and Corbett Scholar at the University of British Columbia. She is an alumna of the University of Washington. *LOVELIKE* is her first full-length poetry collection.

Sah is the 2022–23 Seattle Youth Poet Laureate.
LOVELIKE is her first full-length poetry collection.

Website: sahpham.com
Instagram: sah.pham

This book is set in Garamond Premier Pro

Book design by Cara Sutherland with assistance from
Indira Dahlstrom and Abi Pollokoff

Produced and published by Poetry NW Editions,
an educational press in the Written Arts Program
at Everett Community College